MW00340055

THE BOUNDARIES JOURNAL

THE BOUNDARIES JOURNAL

Prompts and Practices for Healthier Relationships—
and a Happier You

JAIME REEVES, MA, LMFT

ROCKRIDGE
PRESS

Copyright © 2022 by Rockridge Press, Oakland, California

No part of this publication may be reproduced, stored in a retrieval system, or transmitted in any form or by any means, electronic, mechanical, photocopying, recording, scanning, or otherwise, except as permitted under Sections 107 or 108 of the 1976 United States Copyright Act, without the prior written permission of the Publisher. Requests to the Publisher for permission should be addressed to the Permissions Department, Rockridge Press, 1955 Broadway, Suite 400, Oakland, CA 94612.

Limit of Liability/Disclaimer of Warranty: The Publisher and the author make no representations or warranties with respect to the accuracy or completeness of the contents of this work and specifically disclaim all warranties, including without limitation warranties of fitness for a particular purpose. No warranty may be created or extended by sales or promotional materials. The advice and strategies contained herein may not be suitable for every situation. This work is sold with the understanding that the Publisher is not engaged in rendering medical, legal, or other professional advice or services. If professional assistance is required, the services of a competent professional person should be sought. Neither the Publisher nor the author shall be liable for damages arising herefrom. The fact that an individual, organization, or website is referred to in this work as a citation and/or potential source of further information does not mean that the author or the Publisher endorses the information the individual, organization, or website may provide or recommendations they/it may make. Further, readers should be aware that websites listed in this work may have changed or disappeared between when this work was written and when it is read.

For general information on our other products and services or to obtain technical support, please contact our Customer Care Department within the United States at (866) 744-2665, or outside the United States at (510) 253-0500.

Rockridge Press publishes its books in a variety of electronic and print formats. Some content that appears in print may not be available in electronic books, and vice versa.

TRADEMARKS: Rockridge Press and the Rockridge Press logo are trademarks or registered trademarks of Callisto Media Inc. and/or its affiliates, in the United States and other countries, and may not be used without written permission. All other trademarks are the property of their respective owners. Rockridge Press is not associated with any product or vendor mentioned in this book.

Interior and Cover Designer: Darren Samuel
Art Producer: Sue Bischofberger
Editor: Adrian Potts
Production Editor: Jax Berman
Production Manager: Martin Worthington

[Photographer Name/Agency, p.xx (for stock photos); Photographer Name, p.xx (for custom photos] Design note: run cover and interior photo credits together in one paragraph lead with the front and back cover credits, interior credits to follow.
[Photography/Illustrations © Artist name, year] Design note: use for stand-alone custom photo/illustration credit

Paperback ISBN: 978-1-63807-653-7
eBook ISBN: 978-1-63807-883-8
R0

"None of us have simple stories. We are as complex as all of the things that have been done to us."

—ALOK VAID-MENON

CONTENTS

INTRODUCTION

Do you ever look around yourself and feel alone, unseen, drained? Does it seem like you give and give, and never receive? Are you holding on to resentments and anger? Do you feel that life is unfair, and everyone wins but you? If any of that sounds familiar, then you might have an issue with setting and maintaining healthy boundaries.

As a licensed marriage and family therapist, I see this all too often. In my private practice in Los Angeles, I've helped people from all walks of life: single, married, straight, LGBTQIA+, artists, bankers, and so many more. Everyone at some point needs acceptance and support. It's been my privilege to bring that support to many clients over the years, and now I'd like to offer it to you.

"Boundary" is a simple word, but many of us don't really fully understand what it means. In short, a boundary is a guideline we create that dictates how we want to be treated and what we are willing to accept from others—and from ourselves.

It wasn't until I was in college that I really began to notice the consequences of having unhealthy boundaries. The first big eye-opener happened while working on a group project. Instead of saying to my partner, "No, I can't do the whole project and let you put your name on it so you can go out with the third-string point guard," I said, "Yeah! Of course. Have fun!" I didn't respect my time, my resources, or myself, and I set a standard of overextending myself and letting others take advantage of me. Sound familiar?

So yes, that's what an unhealthy boundary looks like. But what is a healthy boundary? The American Psychological Association describes this as a psychological line that protects a person and sets realistic limits in relationships and activities. I would describe a boundary as a personal standard that's reflected in the responses we give to ourselves and others. Boundaries are meant to protect, preserve, and guide you.

HOW TO USE THIS JOURNAL

If you've found your way to this journal, you're ready to explore what it means to use boundaries to actively love and support yourself everywhere life takes you.

Journaling is an easy and effective way to start your personal growth process, explore what's possible, and create plans to achieve it. It can help you learn about yourself and become more self-aware of what's been holding you back. It can help you work through your fears and reimagine the harmful stories we tell ourselves every day.

That said, journaling isn't a substitute for therapy or professional help, so if you are experiencing ongoing worry or sadness, look to the Resources on page 149 for information about finding help. Remember, there is never any shame in reaching out for support.

Each section of this journal contains writing prompts and exercises for you to explore. They'll help direct your thinking to places you might not have found on your own. I suggest progressing through these pages in the order they're written. The sections of the book build on one another, to help you strip down misconceptions (like my college fallacy about boundaries) and effortlessly rebuild a deeper understanding.

In Part I, we'll explore how outside influences contribute to the boundaries we set, even if we don't realize it. In Part II, you'll learn what boundaries really are, how to identify a boundary crossing or violation, and what to do when one occurs. In Part III, we'll discuss how you can better communicate your boundaries and let go of barriers to your well-being, such as guilt and fear. In Part IV, you'll see how boundaries can help nurture a closer relationship with yourself. Finally, to finish this workbook, in Part V, you'll redefine what your new future looks like, and you'll create a plan to maintain what you've learned and continue to grow in confidence. Let's get started!

PART I

Discovering Your Influences

Boundaries don't develop out of nowhere. We learn them from the people, places, and things we cross paths with, the elements that influence us throughout our lives. Those influences can be anything from trauma you experience to cultural customs, family traditions, the neighborhood you grew up in, and the places where you worked or went to school.

Always remember, boundaries are learned. So let's dig deep into what lessons no longer serve you. This is where you get to let go of influences that burden you, and change your story for the better. You'll gain a deeper understanding of how every loss and lesson has helped you grow and get to this point in your journey.

Boundaries are the guidelines we create that dictate how we want to be treated and what we are willing to accept from others and, more importantly, from ourselves. They are a foundation of any healthy relationship. We all need reasonable boundaries that support a life we can thrive in. How would you describe your boundaries at this point in your journey? Try listing and describing the boundaries that are most important to you.

When terrible things happen, we can get stuck in a negative loop. We forget we're still standing. We forget we overcame something that tried to stop us. When this happens, we forget to value who we become as a result of those lessons learned. Reflect on a time when choosing to value your hard-earned growth was difficult but the right thing to do.

What was the lesson you took from that experience?

Sometimes we fail to set a boundary because it can be hard to feel like we're disappointing someone. But it's not always wise to say yes just to avoid conflict or hurt feelings. How often do you say no, even if it feels uncomfortable? Write about an example of when and why you have and how it felt. If nothing comes to mind, write about a time you said yes but regretted it.

It's important to be intentional about what influences you allow into your life. List the people who have been the biggest influences on you during the last year. Where does their influence show up in your day-to-day decision-making? Do you consider these influences to be positive forces in your life?

LOOKING AT CHILDHOOD RULES

Sometimes the rules we grew up with can affect the rules we have with others as adults. Consider the example given here, then fill out the table to examine how rules you learned earlier in life are serving you today.

RULE	WHO TAUGHT ME THIS	LESSON I LEARNED	IS IT STILL HELPFUL?
Family business stays behind closed doors.	Mother and father.	It's okay and encouraged to keep secrets.	No. It makes it hard to get help when I need it.

You have permission to let toxic people go, no matter who they are, if they cause harm or influence you negatively. When it comes to relationships, what behavior do you consider toxic? Do you see any of this in your life, and how can you change it?

HOW DO SOCIAL NORMS AFFECT YOU?

A social norm is a shared and accepted standard of behavior in a group. The norms we observe in our lives often have a big influence on our ability to set boundaries. For example, if you come from a family in which expressing your feelings is seen as a sign of weakness, then you may have trouble letting others know how you feel. Norms usually fall into four categories:

◆ **Cultural norms:** Standards of behavior within your cultural group.
◆ **Family norms:** Acceptable behavior within the family.
◆ **School/work norms:** Organizational rules or standards within an organization.
◆ **Peer norms:** Peer group rules and socially acceptable behavior.

Use this table to write about some norms you have observed, and how they've influenced your boundaries.

Cultural Norms	Family Norms
School/Work Norms	Peer Norms

Thinking about your place of work, or the work you do in your home, write about the boundaries you have or would like to have. For example, this might be saying no to working more than a reasonable number of hours, or not picking up slack for other people without having the same done in return.

Now think about how you feel when people cross your boundaries relating to your work life. Do you feel stressed about confronting someone over this? Do you think it would feel empowering to let people know how you feel?

I choose to release what does not serve me anymore

Sometimes you may feel unable to change the dynamics of long-standing relationships, especially those within your family. However, agency—a sense of self-direction—is something you always have access to. Write about the role(s) you play within your family. Are you the scapegoat, the hero, the golden child, or something else? Is this a role you chose, or was it assigned to you? How do you feel about the role(s)?

Now reflect on what you would like to change in your family dynamics. For example, are there ways in which you would like to be treated with more respect? Do you wish that you could say no more often? Write whatever comes into your mind.

What roles have you played with current or past romantic partners? For example, are you somebody who gets what they want out of intimate connections, or do you find yourself going without in order to please others?

WHAT ARE YOUR EMOTIONAL TRIGGERS?

An emotional trigger is something that sets off a chain reaction in us. We not only reexperience something from the past that was emotionally difficult, the intensity causes us to overcorrect. We react out of alignment with the present moment. When we can identify what triggers us, we can work on how we respond to these situations. Create an inventory of your main triggers:

I become worried when: ....

I become defensive when: ....

I become angry when: ....

I feel guilty when: ....

I freeze up when: ....

I feel ashamed when: ....

I feel uncertain when: ....

We'll work on managing these triggers on the next page.

PRACTICING INTENTIONAL CALM

When we react to stress without an intentional, thoughtful response, we're less likely to make good decisions. Let's work on responding to a trigger with intentional calm.

1. Sit or lie in a comfortable position.

2. Bring to mind an emotional trigger you have and the feeling it evokes. While holding that in your mind, draw in a deep breath and allow your attention to follow that breath as you fill your lungs, breathing deeply through the nose.

3. Gently release your breath through your mouth, allowing your attention to follow your breath as it flows out.

4. Repeat this breathing for 1 minute.

   Observe how you feel about the trigger when you are finished. Has the intensity of the feeling decreased? Practice this technique so it will be easy to access when you need it urgently and under pressure.

We often learn how to set boundaries and create healthy relationship dynamics with others by mimicking what we see. Our role models teach us a lot in this way. Bring to mind an important role model in your life, then write about the boundaries you've created as a result of their influence. Do you consider these boundaries to be healthy? Are there things you want to change?

When it comes to social circle(s), what boundaries do you think are important? Try to include examples you find easy to assert, and some that you would like to work on.

When you were a child, were there certain things adults made you do that you didn't want to do? How did that feel for you then, and how does that affect you now?

When we're overly set in our boundaries, we strangle growth before it can take root. This isn't to be confused with important needs, or physical and sexual boundaries, where clear and decisive rules and limitations are particularly important. Write down 5 to 10 deal-breakers you have for yourself and others when it comes to social inter-actions or trying new things. Are they all reasonable, or are any cutting yourself off from opportunity?

A SENSE OF PRIDE

It's hard to understand how to create boundaries without first feeling proud of who you are. What do you feel proudly expresses your true self? Fill in the blanks.

I feel accomplished when: ....

....

The biggest challenge I have overcome is: ....

....

I am capable of: ....

....

I inspire other people by: ....

....

Reflecting on your answers, think of a single statement that sums up why you are proud of who you are and write it down.

....

....

Now, find a quiet place and declare this statement—out loud or in your head to yourself. If you aren't somewhere private, save this activity for later. Saying who you are with pride can help you cut through negative beliefs and tune in to your inner voice.

We all adjust our behavior based on where we are. You might be subdued at work compared with how vibrant you are at the family cookout. How do you find yourself changing your behavior based on the setting you're in? Do you find it harder to be yourself in certain places?

_____

_____

_____

_____

_____

_____

_____

_____

_____

_____

Being true to your own sense of self, values, and spirit can be scary, but the benefits of being authentic outweigh the hardship. Living an authentic life is hard, but if you can't reveal the truth of who you are, no matter how scary that feels, how will anyone truly know you? Consider a time when you found courage to be yourself or express your true self. How were you able to step up to the challenge?

Facing your vulnerabilities is one of the purest acts of bravery you will ever commit. Tell your victory story: Share a moment where you were brave while facing your fears. How did it feel?

In psychology, "projection" refers to displacing unwanted feelings and fears onto others. For example, we may criticize a trait in somebody else that we secretly find unacceptable in ourselves. This can cloud our judgment and make it harder to know where to draw boundaries. How do you think projection may have affected your ability to set boundaries in past relationships?

In the future, how can you take a step back when you catch yourself projecting? What can you do to see such situations more clearly? How would this help you set clear and fair boundaries with others?

_____

_____

_____

_____

_____

_____

_____

_____

_____

_____

_____

KNOWING YOUR WORTH

Self-esteem refers to a person's overall sense of personal value and self-worth. These beliefs about ourselves are first formed through recurring experiences with the world from a young age and continue to evolve as we age. When we lack self-esteem, it becomes almost impossible to create boundaries in our daily lives, because we don't believe we're worthy of support. When we don't value ourselves, it becomes difficult to hold others to a standard we ourselves don't meet.

To help build your self-esteem, try saying the following affirmations—out loud or in your head to your reflection in the mirror—as you start each day.

- ◆ I am valuable and worthy of love.
- ◆ I am who I am supposed to be, and becoming who I am meant to be.
- ◆ I will do my best today, whatever that looks like.

If you wish, you can write down any affirmations of your own that you want to add to the list.

PART II
Exploring Your Boundaries

Now that you've assessed how past influences affect the boundaries you set, let's focus on the different types of boundaries present in your life and how they function. In doing so, you have the opportunity to edit the standards you live by and reshape the boundaries you hold for yourself and others.

"Boundaries define us. They define what is me and what is not me. A boundary shows me where I end and someone else begins, leading me to a sense of ownership. Knowing what I am to own and take responsibility for gives me freedom."

—HENRY CLOUD

If you think about it, we have boundaries for everything. We have sexual boundaries; boundaries relating to money, relationships, and food; physical and time/energy boundaries. Take some time to write about when and where you would feel comfortable setting and maintaining new, healthier boundaries in different areas of your life.

HOW DO YOU FEEL SETTING BOUNDARIES?

What is your comfort level when it comes to setting boundaries? Answer the following questions.

	Rarely	Sometimes	Often
1. I say yes to things I don't want to do.	☐	☐	☐
2. I try to fix other people's problems.	☐	☐	☐
3. I find it uncomfortable to express my emotions.	☐	☐	☐
4. I feel a sense of obligation to help other people.	☐	☐	☐
5. I feel guilty when I say no to someone.	☐	☐	☐
6. I worry about disappointing or annoying other people by stating my opinion.	☐	☐	☐
7. I find myself accepting poor treatment from others.	☐	☐	☐
8. I agree with other people to avoid conflict.	☐	☐	☐
9. I put the needs and wants of others before my own.	☐	☐	☐
10. I apologize for things that are not my fault.	☐	☐	☐

How did you do? Let's look at your results.

◆ If most of your responses were **rarely**, you are likely already making progress when it comes to setting healthy boundaries.
◆ If most of your responses were **sometimes**, you may have trouble with boundaries in some situations.
◆ If most of your responses were **often**, then you likely face challenges with boundary setting.

No matter what you answered, what matters is that you do your best to accept where you are, to free yourself of judgment about wherever that may be, and to feel reassured that you are doing your best to make positive changes.

Use the following space to write down what comes to mind after doing this exercise. What feelings come up? Do you feel any frustration or shame about a lack of boundaries? How can you be more compassionate to yourself and stay focused on making progress?

Boundaries can be broken into three categories: porous, healthy, and rigid.

- **Porous boundaries** are inconsistent, unclear, and easily crossed. People with porous boundaries focus on the needs of others rather than their own. For example, you may want to go home for the night, but your friends want to bar hop. Instead of calling it a night, you follow the wants of others.
- **Healthy boundaries** are guided by a person's own values, needs, and integrity. They let others know how you wish to be respected. There may come a time when you disagree with a close friend and, despite the possibility of upsetting them, you hold true to your beliefs but stay open to conversation.
- **Rigid boundaries** are hard lines with no exceptions. Sticking to them can sometimes look like standoffishness to others. That said, not every rigid boundary is unhealthy. Context matters a great deal. It would be reasonable to set a rigid boundary around stopping strangers from accessing your bank account or violating your personal space. However, rigid boundaries can become unhealthy in less serious situations when some compromise may be helpful or necessary.

Make a list of two porous, two healthy, and two rigid boundaries you may have, and explain why you put each in that category.

Porous: ....

....

....

Healthy: ....

....

....

Rigid: ....

....

....

By knowing where your porous boundaries lie, you can take action to put healthy boundaries in their place. Think about the porous boundaries you identified in the previous prompt, and write about what steps you can take to turn them into healthy ones.

We exercise our boundaries based on the *values* and *beliefs* we have. Values are ideas we place high importance on, and beliefs are what we accept to be true. Put into words three values and three beliefs that you hold with confidence and conviction, and why.

My values:

My beliefs:

What makes you valuable? It's hard to know how and when to set a boundary if you don't know what your value is. Take some time to describe yourself, focusing on what you admire the most about you.

SHOWING YOUR WORTH

Now let's think about how you show your value to other people. In this table, write what you would like to be valued for, and specifically how you are going to show that valuable quality to other people.

MY VALUABLE QUALITY	HOW I WILL SHOW IT TO OTHERS
Example: My confidence.	Example: I will share my ideas during meetings at work.

A common barrier to setting boundaries is feeling uncomfortable about imposing limits on others. Think of boundaries as acts of self-love. They demonstrate, to yourself and to others, that you understand your worth. Take some time to write about how you express on a daily basis that you value yourself.

....

....

....

....

....

Now reflect on what you would like others to learn from watching how well you treat yourself.

....

....

....

....

....

Respect is an important part of developing healthy boundaries. As you get to know and make peace with yourself, you begin to make it easier for others to know you. And it becomes easier to be peaceful with others. What does it look like to respect yourself?

As you become more comfortable and confident in demonstrating self-respect, it becomes clearer for you when others are being disrespectful to you. Write about a time when others disregarded or disrespected your boundaries. What happened, and how did it make you feel?

_____

_____

_____

_____

_____

_____

_____

_____

_____

_____

There are three ways people tend to cross your boundaries:

- **Testing:** Someone tests a boundary without thought or intent to do harm, but will usually self-correct when you establish your boundary.
- **Crossing:** Somebody crosses a boundary knowingly and needs repeated correction.
- **Violation:** A serious and harmful action that needs immediate correction. You may have to remove yourself entirely from an encounter or relationship when this happens.

Write personal examples of all three on this page.

Let's explore boundary testing some more. Bring to mind a time someone tested your boundaries. For example, say you and a romantic partner attended a party together. Prior to leaving, you have a disagreement. Your partner was insistent about being publicly affectionate. Even though you did not directly express a boundary regarding public displays of affection, it still felt uncomfortable. This could be a test of where the boundaries currently rest.

Now write about your own experience that you brought to mind. Did you notice that the boundary had been tested right away? How did it make you feel? What was your reaction and what was the outcome?

HANDLING BOUNDARY CROSSINGS

When people cross your boundaries, you need to reinforce them. Let's practice. How would you handle these boundary crossings?

1. One of your parents is upset with your sibling. You have asked your parent before to keep you out of their arguments. The parent comes to you to vent and complain about your sibling. Your response:

   a) Refuse to discuss it altogether.
   b) Agree with their complaints to end the discussion.
   c) Respectfully remind them that you don't want to be involved.

2. Your friend has a habit of not returning what they borrow. After a study session you notice that your notes from school are missing and later find them in your friend's possession. Your response:

   a) Move on and never mention it again.
   b) Cut off ties with the friend.
   c) Request that they ask you before they take something.

3. You have stated in the past that you dislike surprises. Your significant other surprises you with a last-minute plan to have dinner with friends, leaving you anxious. Your response:

   a) Reaffirm that you don't enjoy last-minute plans, and ask for more notice in the future.
   b) Don't show up to dinner.
   c) Pretend that noting is bothering you so you don't spoil the evening.

How did you do? Let's look at the answers.

- **Healthy:** If you answered 1 c, 2 c, and 3 a, you are on your way to having healthy boundaries that you can reinforce.
- **Porous:** If you answered 1 b, 2 a, and 3 c, you may be prone to having more porous boundaries. Consider how you could respond differently in each situation to better reinforce your boundaries.
- **Rigid:** If you answered 1 a, 2 b, and 3 b, it's possible your boundaries are very rigid and may be so inflexible that they distance you from others. Consider if different responses to each situation might lead to a more conciliatory outcome.

Use this space to reflect on what comes to mind after doing this exercise. Are there certain situations in which you find it easier to reinforce your boundaries? What areas do you want to work on?

When you knowingly or unknowingly cross someone else's boundaries, do you feel the need to make amends? How do you do it? Explain your answer.

_____

_____

_____

_____

_____

Do you expect others to make amends when they cross your boundaries? Why or why not?

_____

_____

_____

_____

_____

The third state of a compromised boundary is the boundary violation, the most severe situation. This occurs when someone knowingly prioritizes their wants and needs at another's expense. An example would be you telling your parent you saved $500, and they take the money from you "because you don't need it." How might you respond when someone violates your boundaries?

Finding yourself in relationships where boundary crossings and violations happen frequently could be a sign that there is something out of alignment. Take a moment to do inventory on your past and current relationships. Who has been a positive force, and who has been a drain on your energy? Explain why they fall into each category.

Are you a reactor or a responder in stressful situations? To react is to be impulsive, acting on emotion or habit. To respond is to be intentional and thoughtful in your actions. Write about what you tend to do in times of stress, and whether this may help or hinder your ability to set boundaries.

My value is not defined by what I do,
but by who I am.

When deciding when to set a boundary, try leading with compassion for both yourself and others. Compassion can be defined as a willingness to extend kindness without the expectation of having it returned. When we set boundaries with compassion, our intention isn't to control or punish, it is to guide and support. What do you think of when you think of the word "compassion"? List up to 10 ways you show compassion to yourself and others daily.

We crave connection to others for a variety of reasons, one of which is isolation and loneliness. Have you ever tolerated mistreatment by someone in order to hold on to the connection you have? If so, explain in detail why you made that decision. If not, what happens to your connection to someone if you're feeling mistreated by them?

_____

_____

_____

_____

_____

_____

_____

_____

_____

_____

_____

SETTING YOUR BOUNDARIES

It can help to think of the following four steps when establishing boundaries.

1. **Define:** Know your boundary and why you are setting it.

2. **Communicate:** Make your boundary clear if it is overstepped.

3. **Keep it simple:** Don't overexplain why you have this boundary. Remember that everyone has the right to decide what they will and won't do.

4. **Set consequences:** Say what will happen if the boundary is not respected in the future. Remember, being assertive doesn't have to mean being threatening.

Think of a boundary you would like to set, then fill out the following table to put the steps into action.

Define: Describe your boundary and desired outcome.	
Communicate: Write what you would say to make your boundary clear.	
Keep it simple: Is your statement simple and direct? If not, try revising it.	
Set consequences: Write what consequence(s) you set if the boundary is not being respected.	

We use a lot of energy trying to ward off other people's displeasure and anticipate how to give them what they want and need at an unreasonable cost to ourselves. On the flip side, we can be the ones making unreasonable demands of others. Have you noticed either of these behaviors in yourself? Do you think you get anything positive out of it?

PUTTING YOURSELF FIRST

When we focus more on others than on ourselves, we tend to make decisions that don't align with what we really want. Review the table on this page, which provides examples of choices made based on the needs or opinions of others. Write how you could set a boundary if you were in the same situation.

THE OTHER PERSON	THE SITUATION	HOW I COULD SET A BOUNDARY
Boss	I say yes to staying late, then feel resentment for it.	
Friend	They insist I am a bad friend if I do not go out tonight, so I go but hate it.	
Partner	They dislike my hobbies, so I give them up and feel angry.	
Family Member	They insist I am ungrateful when I disagree with their actions, so I do as they ask.	

Setting boundaries doesn't make you a mean person, and honoring another's boundaries doesn't mean you're being punished or controlled. We have to weigh each request against our own set of values and beliefs, and find middle ground. In this way, boundaries are an intentional collaboration, to work collectively toward shared wholeness in fulfilled needs. What comes to mind when you think about this process?

List a handful of key skills you think you need to effectively collaborate in this way.

Now that you have listed skills that have helped you collaborate with others to create a balanced healthy relationship, list the ways you have learned to interact with people that has caused disharmony in your past relationships.

While having compassion for others is important, giving too much of it can lead to compassion burnout. This can result in our not taking care of ourselves, being less aware of our needs, feeling more frustrated, and becoming emotionally drained. Do you think you have ever felt compassion burnout? What caused it? How did it express itself?

A MEDITATION TO CLEAR YOUR MIND

A body scan meditation is a good way to promote self-awareness, notice your feelings, and reduce stress levels. In times of worry, it can help to take 5 or 10 minutes out of your day to do a scan like this.

1. Sit or lie in a comfortable position.

2. Take a few deep breaths in and out.

3. Starting at your feet and slowly moving up to the crown of your head, focus your attention on each area of your body.

4. As you scan, notice any sensations present. You may like to give thanks for each body feature and what it does for you.

5. If you notice any areas of tension, take a deep breath in and out, and imagine that part of the body relaxing.

6. If you find yourself having critical and negative thoughts, notice and observe without judgment, and bring your attention back to the exercise.

7. When you are finished, take a moment to notice how you feel.

It can help to do this exercise when you are making decisions about your boundaries, in order to clear your mind and reduce anxiety.

PART III

Addressing Anxiety, Guilt, and Fear

As we've seen, there are multiple factors that affect our ability to set boundaries. This part of your workbook will help guide you to make healthy decisions by making amends, taking accountability, and processing any guilt, fear, or anxiety you're holding on to. You'll begin to let go of whatever's keeping you from being the best version of yourself.

"You may not control all the events that happen to you, but you can decide not to be reduced by them."

—MAYA ANGELOU

Our boundaries can change depending on whom they relate to. For example, you may be happy with a hug from a close family member or friend, but not want to be hugged by someone you just met. Do you have a boundary that changes depending on the person you're around? Explain why that might be.

Sometimes we let another person cross a boundary to avoid negative feelings, like fear. You may be scared of letting them down, worry about their reaction, or be fearful of conflict. Write about how you experience anxiety around boundaries. Try to express yourself freely, and hold back any judgment about your choices.

It can be hard to make smart decisions when you're stressed. Everyone responds differently. For some of us, stress affects our appetite; for others, stress makes us feel unbelievably tired. Some people become very sad and find it hard to make decisions. How do you recognize stress when it shows up in your daily life? How do you respond?

Valuing yourself on your own terms, rather than by how other people value you, is important for a sense of self-worth and self-esteem. While it's not wise to live in a bubble, it's equally unwise to rely solely on others to define your worth for you. For example, if you set a boundary and someone tells you you're being unreasonable, you'll want to consider what they're saying, but not automatically sacrifice your own needs or comforts to please them. Share what this balance between inner and outer validation looks like for you.

MANTRAS FOR EMOTIONAL WELL-BEING

Here are five mantras for emotional well-being. Try reciting these in your head, or out loud to yourself, and notice how you feel afterward.

1. I take care of my needs, so I can show up for others I care about.

2. I don't hold on to the past, but I learn from it.

3. I release false modesty. I don't make myself smaller to accommodate another's ego.

4. I am my own best friend. I speak kindly to myself, especially when I make a mistake.

5. I accept that life is about change and requires me to adjust and be flexible about how I move forward in the face of hardship or disappointment.

Challenge yourself to recite these each day in the coming week. You might keep them in the notes app of your phone or post them in your personal space at work, so you can remember and recite them whenever you need them.

The need to control is a natural response to discomfort and fear. Sadly, this instinct only seems to make things worse, because there's so much we can't control. But we can choose to act on what we do, say, and believe. When someone does something that isn't in alignment with your expectations, how do you typically respond? How do you want to respond?

The "critical I" is the part of us that places a harsh view on everything we do or try to do. It speaks to us negatively, telling us things like, "You can't do that," or "Everyone will laugh at you." The critical I keeps us from expressing ourselves honestly or attempting something new. In the coming week, try doing something unexpected and at least a little outside your comfort zone. Set aside your embarrassment and just be yourself. When you're done, come back to this journal and explore how it felt to ignore the "critical I."

To follow endless thoughts of the past is to fall into regret. To focus intently on the future as if it is being lived *now* is to be anxious. Staying in the present, to take healthy action and allow yourself to enjoy your present life, is key. What do you imagine it feels like to loosen your hold on both the past and future, and enjoy right now?

BREATH AWARENESS FOR CALM

Breath awareness is a great way to center yourself and reduce anxiety. Here's how to do it:

1. Sit or lie in a comfortable position.

2. Check in with your body. Do you feel any areas of tension? Notice your breath. Are you holding it? Is it shallow? Is your breathing fast or slow?

3. Allow yourself to be still, putting your feet flat on the ground (if you're sitting) and resting your palms face up on your thighs. Now take a deep, gentle breath, pulling fresh air in and up.

4. Imagine your breath reaching to the top of your head, then slowly release. As you let go of your breath, allow your body to deflate as you let the air out.

5. Repeat for up to 5 to 10 minutes at a comfortable pace.

When you are finished, observe how you feel compared with when you started. Deep-breathing practices like this can be a useful go-to if you find yourself caught up in worry.

Sometimes we forgo setting boundaries with others because we feel guilty doing so. You may feel bad that you're prioritizing your needs over someone else's. Has there been a time you struggled with guilt when setting a boundary with someone you care about?

How do you think you may have acted differently if you thought of setting the boundary as a form of taking care of yourself, rather than being selfish?

_____

_____

_____

_____

_____

_____

_____

_____

_____

_____

_____

When we're feeling guilty, we can harm ourselves out of a misguided attempt to "make things right." For example, Maria's rent is due, and she has just enough to cover it. A friend reminds her that they loaned her money months ago. Maria gives the friend her rent money rather than feel guilty, regardless of the consequences to herself.

How have you, or someone close to you, been self-destructive because of guilt? What did you notice about your own experience?

I am stronger and more beautiful because of what I have come through.

Triggers, as we learned earlier, are very reactive. When a trigger affects us, we react to pain we felt in the past more than to anything we're feeling in the present moment. Think about a time when you reacted to a trigger, anticipating emotional pain before it happened.

_____

_____

_____

_____

_____

_____

_____

_____

_____

Resentment and fear can cause people to set boundaries out of anger, with the intention to manipulate, control, or punish. Have you ever done this to someone? Have you been on the receiving end? What were your experiences like?

REFRAMING YOUR SELF-TALK

Sometimes by reframing how you talk to yourself, you can free yourself from unhelpful narratives that keep you stuck. Try this by thinking of some things you wish you were better at. For example, maybe you tell yourself, "I am terrible at speaking in front of other people." Then flip that around into a positive statement: "I want to share something that matters to me with other people." Try this approach to reframe three negative beliefs.

Negative belief: ....

....

Positive statement: I want to ....

....

Negative belief: ....

....

Positive statement: I want to ....

....

Negative belief: ....

....

Positive statement: I want to ....

....

When we're resentful, we tend to punish other people for crimes and transgressions they had nothing to do with, as if they can make amends for someone else who wronged us. What resentments have you been holding on to in your life? Reflect on how they might be affecting your other relationships.

When we find ourselves having the same issues in relationships with different people, it might be a result of seeking out a corrective experience. Unknowingly, we put ourselves into dysfunctional situations thinking that this time we can fix the problem and have a better outcome. Think about recurring patterns in your past and current relationships. Is something playing on repeat?

How good is your assumption radar? Can you honestly predict what other people need and want? It's doubtful anyone is accurate at this 100 percent of the time, or even close to it. What are some ways that you can be sure your assumptions about others are correct? Start by asking questions: "I'm not sure I understand, can you explain a little more?" How else could you get clarification?

We place all sorts of self-defeating obstacles in front of ourselves. They keep us from growing into our "possible self," a conception of whom we want to be but are afraid to become. Sometimes being awesome can be scary, and we can doubt our ability to make our dreams come true. What is your possible self? Write down three steps you can take to get closer to making that self a reality.

Guilt lets us know that something is off, that we have stepped too far away from our values. Sometimes when we feel guilty about saying no to someone, it's not about the boundary at all. It could be the way you set the boundary that is making you feel guilty. Boundaries aren't meant to harm; they are loving actions. Try setting yours with that in mind, instead of out of anger or frustration.

For example, suppose your close friend only calls you to vent, but never has time to support you. You might be tempted to cut off communication. But instead, you could set a boundary that enables the two of you to connect during good times, not just the bad. Write about a time you set a boundary because it helped both you and the other person.

A boundary doesn't have to be associated with negative feelings. For example, if you tell someone, "I don't loan out money, I give gifts," you're showing love and care for both parties. You protect yourself by not giving away more than you can spare, and the other person isn't burdened with a loan hanging over their head. Consider the emotional boundaries you find hard to set. Can you turn any into loving actions?

Thinking through the ways you can honor your boundaries can help you enact them in real life. Bring to mind an important boundary and answer the following questions about it.

1. What do I need in order to honor this boundary?

....

....

2. What are three steps I can take to gain what I need?

....

....

3. When I reflect on those steps, how do I feel about them?

....

....

If you feel anxious or uncomfortable about the steps you've identified, there is a chance you need to revise the steps so they are simple and effective. Try breaking your need down into smaller parts if you can't achieve it in three steps.

....

....

BEYOND WORDS

There are three elements that are guaranteed to influence your perception of a moment: you, the other person, and the nonverbal cues. In fact, research has found that only 7 percent of our communication is actually conveyed with words. Nonverbal elements including tone, facial expressions, gestures, body language, posture, eye contact, and physical proximity or relation often convey much more.

In the table on the next page you can explore how this plays out in real life. Bring to mind two situations when you tried to have an important or difficult conversation that went nowhere fast. There is space to write about your thoughts and feelings in each situation, how the other person reacted, the nonverbal communication used, and the outcome of the situation. In the final row, you can brainstorm useful changes to the way you communicate nonverbally.

Write out your internal thoughts and feelings about it in row one, the other person's behavior in row two, and a description of nonverbal communication cues in row three. Describe the outcome in row four, and in row five add an alternative nonverbal communication cue that might have improved the situation.

	EXAMPLE SITUATION	MY SITUATION 1	MY SITUATION 2
What I Felt and Thought	I felt angry and that I wasn't being heard.		
How the Other Person Reacted	They appeared frustrated and raised their voice.		
Nonverbal Communication	I was sitting and they were standing over me.		
The Outcome of the Conversation	They talked over me, and we did not reach a resolution.		
Alternative Nonverbal Communication	If we have the conversation again, I could stand up or invite the person to sit down first.		

PART IV

Loving and Accepting Yourself

Boundaries protect us, and to set healthy boundaries, we have to believe we're worth protecting. In Part IV of this workbook, we're going to focus on the importance of self-love, letting go of negative self-talk, and embracing a loving confidence that supports your ability to choose healthy connections. The way that you treat yourself is a model for others to follow in how they treat you.

"Daring to set boundaries is about having the courage to love ourselves, even when we risk disappointing others."

—BRENÉ BROWN

Now that you have explored so much of what makes a healthy boundary, do you have a different view of who you are? Can you separate from what you have created to please others, and see what pleases you? Who are you when you make yourself the priority? Write your thoughts here.

Self-esteem includes confidence in one's worth and abilities. Describe the last time you felt confident in yourself. Why do you think that was?

Our boundaries can be a form of self-love in action. When we show ourselves love, we're showing others how they should respect the way we think and feel. What does self-love look like in your life? How does it influence the way that others treat you?

To accept who we are, we need to know who we are. We have two primary ways we internalize our identity.

◆ The **doing self** is how you identify yourself through your actions: "I am a lawyer" or "I am a workaholic." The doing self's value lasts only as long as you can excel and maintain this activity.

◆ The **being self** is *what* you are beyond your actions. For example, "At my core, I am accepting of my faults and do not judge myself harshly."

How do you define your being self? Do you accept who you are? Use positive statements to describe your being self.

EMBRACING SELF-LOVE

Mind mapping is a creative way to help you brainstorm your wants and needs. On the next page is a mind map template with "self-love" in the center. In the four main boxes that extend from the center, write down a word or phrase that describes an important way you can show yourself self-love. For example, you might write, "Enjoying downtime." Then write down three specific and actionable things you can do to put that into practice. For the example given here, you could write: "Read each night before bed," "Do yoga once a week," and "Spend time with loved ones."

SELF-LOVE

When we doubt ourselves and our value, our goals can feel out of reach. However, sometimes acting "as if" can jump-start you in creating what you have always wanted. Try this by writing about something in your life that feels beyond your reach. An example might be: "I want love myself more unconditionally."

_____

_____

_____

_____

Now, flip that statement, and write about acting as if this wish were already happening. For example, if you wish to love yourself more unconditionally, you might write, "I will commit to acting as if I love myself unconditionally in my thoughts and feelings."

_____

_____

_____

_____

GIVING YOURSELF CREDIT

Write out what you admire about being you.

1. I am happiest when I: _____.

2. I am grateful for: _____.

3. I am inspired by: _____.

4. I am proud of how I: _____.

5. I admire that I can: _____.

6. I am talented at: _____.

7. I trust myself most when: _____.

8. I am strongest when: _____.

9. I am at ease with change when: _____.

10. I am kind to myself when: _____.

It isn't always easy to live up to the idea of our best self. Imagining you have no limitations on what's possible, write about what changes you can make in your life to be more aligned with your best self.

_____

_____

_____

_____

_____

Take this a step further by writing down up to five actions you will take this week to be your best self.

_____

_____

_____

_____

_____

IN WITH THE NEW . . .

In order to create healthy boundaries, we sometimes need to make room for them. Here's an exercise to use when you feel that anxieties and negative memories are keeping you from making a new boundary or reconsidering an old one.

1. Find a comfortable, relaxed position, sitting or lying down. Close your eyes and let your hands fall to your sides. Allow your body to relax and your thoughts to float by like leaves caught in a gentle breeze.

2. As you inhale, draw in love. As you exhale, release fear.

3. Allow yourself to connect to what these emotions feel like for you, and feel them flow through you as you draw in love and release your fears.

4. Continue the exercise for as long as you like.

When we act as if we love others more than we love ourselves, we can end up in a tough situation. We might think we are being loving, but what we are really doing is inaccurately teaching others how to love us. Or rather, we're demonstrating how to fall short of loving us, because we don't tell or show them what we need. Close your eyes and visualize what it feels like to be loved and accepted. Write about what the experience was like.

Regardless of it being intentional or conscious on our part, we connect with others with an expectation of reciprocation. We at times will do something nice in hopes the gesture will be returned.

List four people from whom you hold unspoken expectations of reciprocation, and describe what those expectations are.

_____

_____

_____

_____

Now consider what you could accept if you knew none of those expectations were going to be met. Explore how you might express your needs more clearly.

_____

_____

_____

_____

I have no losses, only lessons.

Self-acceptance is a pathway to freedom. It liberates us from doubt and fortifies us when we face loss or failure. If we instead rely solely on others to validate us and define who we are, we can become confused and full of uncertainty. Reflect on your relationship with self-acceptance. Have you given too much space in yourself to others' definitions of who you are and could be? What have others told you, or implied, that you're supposed to be? Have you told yourself any of these things? Is this who you really are?

None of us can escape change. However, healthy boundaries provide us with stability to help navigate those changes. Write about what boundaries you need to maintain stability and to stay grounded when change occurs.

FRIENDLY REMINDERS

When it comes to making a positive change in your life, it can be helpful to have reminders of how you would like to achieve it. Gather five index cards or blank pieces of paper, and on the front of each, write one thing you know to be true. This might be, "I am a good person at heart." Then on the reverse side of each, write down three things you can do to grow or expand on that truth when it comes to your boundaries. For example:

- Act with integrity.
- Be honest about my boundaries.
- Only give what I can give.

Keep these somewhere handy—like on a bedside table—and pick one up each day to read to yourself, to remind yourself of the changes you would like to make.

Use this space to brainstorm any ideas you have.

An important way to care for yourself is to surround yourself with people who wish you the best. Be protective over whom you allow to be an influence in your life. Do you have friends, family, or maybe a partner who quietly or covertly chip away at you? How do they make you feel in those moments?

....

....

....

....

....

How can you better assert yourself with this person? What would you like to say in moments when they dismiss you or put you down? How can you express that they're crossing a boundary?

....

....

....

....

....

UNIQUELY YOU

If we want to experience self-love in its totality, we have to learn to love, celebrate, and honor the things that make us stand out and apart from others. Use this chart to describe your uniqueness and how you plan to embrace it.

I'M UNIQUELY ...	I EMBRACE THIS BY ...
Capable of being true to myself.	Telling the truth even when it doesn't benefit me.

Gratitude helps us stay connected to our better selves and remember why it's worth honoring boundaries that are sometimes a challenge to assert. It can be difficult to not give way to judgmental thinking, harsh criticism, and doubt. And those are moments when we're tempted to ignore a boundary crossing instead of speaking up for ourselves. When you find yourself in this state, try repeating to yourself: "I'm so grateful I get to . . . " "I'm glad I can . . . " Can you come up with five more affirming statements of gratitude?

Most people see the world from an "I" perspective, considering only their own needs, and not intending to be hurtful when they step on your boundaries to get what they want. Before you react to a perceived slight or hurt, think to yourself: Despite how this person is communicating, how do I want to react? Write about a time somebody crossed your boundary because they were preoccupied by their own needs or unaware of what your boundaries were. How could understanding things from their perspective help you depersonalize the situation and respond more understandingly?

Hard times come to all of us in life. However, we can set boundaries with ourselves about how we choose to react to difficult experiences. Reflect on how you typically respond during tough times. Do you feel anger, resentment, or other negative emotions, or do you seek to accept what you cannot change? Explore what you normally do when things go wrong, and compare that to what you would like to do moving forward.

Happiness is infectious, just as misery is. What do you spread when you are out in the world? Describe the last time you made a stranger smile in your presence, and when your angry or sad mood spread to others. Which of these versions of yourself do you most want to be?

All the feelings you have are valid. Negative feelings are not your enemy or something to be changed. But if we try to deny or ignore them, they grow stronger. Feel them, understand them, *accept* them, and move on to making the next best action for you. If a boundary violation offends or frightens you, acknowledge that feeling, and it will be easier to respond in a healthy way. Has there been a time when you were upset or disappointed and decided to redirect your attention to where you could make a positive change? What helped you do that? How can you do more of it?

WAYS TO STAY GROUNDED

Grounding is how we immediately connect ourselves to the present moment. Feeling grounded is a useful state to be in when you need to make tough decisions, as the present is the only place where you can create change. When we are calm and grounded, we can advocate for ourselves more thoughtfully and effectively. Consider practicing a grounding activity daily so you always have access to a calm state of being. On this page is a list of common grounding activities. How many are you familiar with? Do you use any on a regular basis? What can you add to the list?

1. Yoga

2. Meditation

3. Walking

4. Working out

5. Playing your favorite music

_____

_____

_____

_____

_____

_____

Feelings are not facts. For example, if someone feels hopeless, it does not mean that there's no hope, or that they should behave as if there isn't. When confronted with uncomfortable feelings, we have room to create a response. Bring to mind a time you experienced strong negative feelings. How did those feelings influence your thoughts or self-beliefs?

How could you have challenged or changed your response to those feelings?

PERFECTLY IMPERFECT

We are all perfectly imperfect. That is what makes you so wonderfully unique. When we cast that truth aside, we're inviting shame or embarrassment about our imperfections, rather than accepting and celebrating the things that make us different.

In the coming days, try one of the actions from this list to embrace being imperfect.

1. Be courageous. Do something you're not good at, without caring how it will turn out.

2. Be vulnerable. Share something you feel embarrassed about with a loved one.

3. Tell on yourself. Own up to a mistake you made, without judging yourself.

4. Embrace integrity. Speak your truth, even if you aren't sure others will agree.

5. Open up. Ask someone for help with a problem you have.

When you stand in your perfectly imperfect truth, you'll find it easier to stand up for who you are, rather than trying to please others.

PART V

Maintaining Your Boundaries

We've come to the final part of the journal, and you've likely put in some hard work to get to this point. So we'll close out our time together by considering the ways you can maintain all you have learned and explored thus far. You'll also learn how to respect other people's boundaries, breaking the toxic cycle of harm: When we honor someone else's boundaries, they're more likely to honor ours.

"Mistakes are a fact of life. It is the response to the error that counts."

—NIKKI GIOVANNI

Burnout is the biggest enemy to maintaining all your hard-earned progress. When you are exhausted, you're more likely to minimize your problems, judge yourself harshly, feel self-doubt and helplessness, and lose your motivation, among other things. Consider what burnout feels like for you, and list the warning signs that you're approaching burnout.

Sometimes it becomes necessary to give our boundaries a little spring cleaning. Think for a moment about the boundaries you have been holding on to that are no longer helpful. List three habits that no longer serve you in your current life. How do you want to change them? What would you replace them with?

It's unavoidable that you will have moments when you want to take a pause and reflect on where you're at with yourself and in your relationships. Consider that regardless of your motivation level, there is always something you can do to support yourself. Describe what self-care looks like for you in the following scenarios.

When I am tired and low on motivation, I can still practice self-care by:

....

....

....

When I am content, I can practice self-care by:

....

....

....

When I am motivated, I can practice self-care by:

....

....

....

When we respect our values, we commit to following them to honor ourselves. For example, by telling the truth even if it disappoints someone we love. When was the last time you did the right thing by your values, even when it was inconvenient or difficult?

THE PRESENT SELF

Your past self is a teacher, your future self is a dreamer, but your present self is a creator. Being present-focused is where you are most powerful: You can make decisions and take action in the present. The next time you feel pulled off track or distracted, perhaps tempted to devalue your needs or boundaries, try this 5-4-3-2-1 method for a hard reset.

- Look at your surroundings, and name **five** things that catch your eye. Explore the visual details as much as you can.
- Now run your hands over **four** things you can touch. Notice the textures and sensations of each.
- Next, listen to **three** things you can hear. Try to isolate the sounds as you notice them.
- Notice **two** things you can smell, paying attention to the distinct qualities of each scent.
- Finally, notice **one** emotion you are currently feeling. Don't judge it, just notice.

When you're finished, observe how you feel more connected to the moment than to worries about the past or projections about the future.

Sometimes you will meet people who don't value themselves and in turn find it hard to value you. This does not mean we lower our standards to treat them poorly. Instead, we exercise the boundaries that support our standards and operate with integrity. What does that look like for you?

Integrity is something we maintain when no one is watching. We maintain standards even if they cost us. For example, I strive to be kind in my honesty even if it is not expedient. Describe what integrity means to you. Do your boundaries reflect your definition of integrity?

Are you good at reading people? If you find yourself walking away from a relationship dissatisfied or in conflict with others, you may not be as intuitive as you think. Instead of trying to "read" people like a magic trick, try asking for clarification next time. When have your predictive powers failed you? What clarification could you have asked for instead?

When we have expectations that are not met by someone, we often take it personally and assume they don't respect us. That isn't always the case. How often have you been so preoccupied with your own needs that you failed to meet the needs of others, perhaps crossing a boundary in the process? How common is it for others to make the same mistake?

RESPECTING THE BOUNDARIES OF OTHERS

As we learn how to communicate and maintain our boundaries, we also have to learn to respect the boundaries of others. If you feel resistance to respecting other people's boundaries, or feel guilt or confusion when others set boundaries with you, remind yourself of these five truths:

1. I am allowed to say no without explanation or justification.

2. I can change my mind if a situation no longer feels right for me.

3. I am not a mind reader and will get things wrong sometimes.

4. I have the right to be and feel different.

5. Understanding does not mean agreement—I can respectfully disagree.

Reflect on these statements and how you feel about each one. Then repeat them out loud or in your head, each time replacing "I" with "other people" or the name of a person whose boundaries are a problem for you. For example: For number 1, you could say, "Other people are allowed to say no without explanation or justification."

I can have my needs met
while being compassionate and kind.

Prioritizing yourself isn't selfish, even if others perceive it as such. It takes courage and wisdom to make sure your roots are strong before using your branches to pull others up. When was the last time you put yourself first, even if you worried that others would judge you? How can you do this again in the future?

Holding your boundaries and respecting those of others is a simple choice but not always easy in practice. Can you think of a time when you made a simple choice to do the right thing in respecting someone, then had to struggle to follow through with that choice? What helped you hold to your decision? What were the benefits of your choice? Describe your experience here.

KEEPING MOTIVATED

Though it's a simple decision to keep up with your healthy boundaries, maintaining them can wear you down from time to time. When you notice it's getting hard for you to get out of bed, or your motivation is waning, it can help to shake up your morning routine. Try these three simple ways to kickstart your day:

1. Wake up 15 to 30 minutes early.

2. Make your bed once you're up.

3. Spend some time stretching or doing some exercise you like, such as yoga or taking a walk.

4. Before you look at your phone or turn on the TV, take three deep breaths and repeat an empowering affirmation for the day ten times. You can choose an affirmation from this book, or think up your own.

The best thing you can do for the people you care about, and for yourself, is to tend to your own garden. We want to give the best of ourselves to those we love, not the stressed or angry versions of ourselves. What do you need to do for yourself more often, to ensure you share the best you have to give?

When we obsess over perfection, we end up complicating our lives. The most valuable lesson to learn is knowing how much effort is enough, even if a task doesn't feel complete. Sometimes we can only do what we can and leave the rest for later. When have you pushed yourself too hard? What was the consequence? How can you be kinder to yourself and more comfortable with doing enough?

Dealing with boundary crossings and violations in the moment is a good standard to uphold. Although, as with all things, there are exceptions. One is when you are not up to the task. Perhaps you are tired or uncertain how you feel. It's okay to say, to yourself or to the other person involved, "I didn't like that, but I need time to think about how I feel." Do you find it difficult to admit you need time to think? Is it unbearable to wait to address an issue? If so, why?

TAKING A PAUSE

When you feel overwhelmed, or as if there were a wave of urgency flowing over you, that is anxiety. Even as you get better at setting and maintaining your boundaries, it's possible you will still feel some anxiety. That's okay! Anxiety is nothing more than a warning system, letting you know that an action needs to be taken. You don't have to rush to answer the call every time. In fact, I want you to pause when you feel urgency in a nonthreatening situation, and take these steps.

1. **Ground yourself.** Find an object that's close by and describe it to yourself in detail. Slow your breathing, and let your mind and body settle down.

2. **Make a small change**. Take a small action to help reset your thoughts and feelings. Are you sitting? Try standing up. Do you need to put space between you and another person? Excuse yourself to use the bathroom.

3. **Bring your attention back to the issue at hand.** Now that you are more grounded, what do you feel you need to do? Let your boundaries guide you on your next best step.

By respecting ourselves, we show respect for others. Think about a time someone you know was acting in poor judgment. Did you go along with them, potentially causing you both harm? Or did you demonstrate through your actions the standards you wanted them to connect with? Describe the situation and your feelings about it.

As you begin to set and maintain healthier boundaries, you may feel like an oddball at times. It might even feel lonely at first, as the people in your life adjust to the new you. Take a moment to acknowledge that not everyone will like your self-respect, confidence, and ability to take the lead. Instead of focusing on them, focus on the people who show genuine interest in collaborating with you to build a more balanced and harmonious relationship. Take inventory of how your relationships are evolving, and how you can focus on the healthy ones.

STAYING ON TOP OF "WHAT IFS"

When it comes to maintaining your boundaries, you may find that "what ifs" start to creep into your mind. *What if I look stupid? What if I annoy people?* The next time you catch yourself thinking "What if," try to complete a sentence with the opposite of your fear. Practice with the examples that follow, and add your own. Notice how opposite thinking leads to more positive feelings and provides more confidence.

NEGATIVE THOUGHT	OPPOSITE THOUGHT
Example: What if they don't like me?	Example: What if I am liked and respected?
What if they get upset?	What if ...
What if I embarrass myself?	What if ...
What if they disagree with me?	What if ...
What if I get nervous?	What if ...
What if ...	What if ...
What if ...	What if ...

In order to maintain your growth, you have to make the tough decision to let some fears, and possibly even some people, go. Write a Dear John letter to them in this space and wish them well.

DAILY SELF-CARE

Self-care helps you better cope with stress and prioritize what's important to you—both of which will be important to maintain healthy boundaries in the long run. To help you make self-care a daily priority, write out some activities that you enjoy on strips of paper, and place them in a jar or container. Some examples might be:

◆ Going for a walk.
◆ Listening to music.
◆ Tending to my hobby.

When you feel uncertain, burned out, or just uninspired, pull a strip from your self-care jar. Commit to doing that activity, even if just for 10 to 15 minutes.

Use this space to brainstorm any ideas you have.

MUTUAL RESPECT

Don't aim to simply treat others the way you want to be treated. Treat them how *they* want to be treated while still honoring how *you* want to be treated.

Bring to mind someone you've had boundary issues with in the past. In the left-hand column, describe ways that they want to be treated, as best as you can tell. In the other column, write about how you want to be treated in relation to each item.

HOW THEY WANT TO BE TREATED	HOW I WANT TO BE TREATED
Example: They expect I will spend all my free time with them.	Example: I need time to myself to recharge.

Now, for each entry on the previous page, write about where your preferences and theirs meet and where you differ. What would it look like to strike a healthy balance in each instance?

What makes you happy? Everyone has a unique way of creating happy moments in their life. How do you create yours?

Healthy boundaries can help you maintain peace. To be peaceful in your life is to face adversity with sure and steady footing, while never drifting too far away from who you are. Who are you when you are peaceful? How do your boundaries enable you to be that person?

Even as you become more comfortable asserting yourself, there will always be times when others cross the line. Do some contingency planning for this by answering the following prompts. Feel free to add to or change the prompts to match your situation.

If I catch my significant other lying to me, I will: _____

_____

If my boss wants me to do more work than what is reasonable, I will: _____

_____

_____

If my friend always cancels our plans, I will: _____

_____

If my family member puts me down, I will: _____

_____

If my friend only reaches out to me when they need something, I will: _____

_____

If my significant other is always canceling plans with me, I will: _____

_____

MOVING FORWARD

Keeping your boundaries strong is going to take effort. The following affirmations remind you that it's okay to set and maintain healthy boundaries as you move forward in your journey.

- I have a right to be heard and take up space.
- I can say no without needing to explain myself.
- Boundaries help me stay true to who I am.
- I can love without being responsible for the happiness of others.
- I deserve respect and safety.
- I have a right to my feelings, regardless of the validation of others.
- How others react or behave is often a reflection of themselves and not me.
- I can set boundaries even when I am overwhelmed or fearful.
- I can let go of the guilt that keeps me in caretaker mode.
- I am enough.

A FINAL WORD

Smile! You did it! You made it through to the other side of this book. But you have only just scratched the surface of all there is to know and love about you. You'll find it easier to pursue that self-knowledge now that you have a basic understanding of how boundaries protect you, keep you safe, and connect you to the people, places, and things you love.

This is just the beginning of your journey, one you can follow while empowered to stand in your truth, speak your mind, and stay aligned with your heart. Take a moment to appreciate what you accomplished. With your hand over your heart, draw a deep breath in, and slowly release it. As you do that, allow your body to relax, and repeat these words: I am worthy of respect. I am worthy of being seen. I am worthy of setting standards and boundaries that reflect the fullest expression of who I am. I am worthy.

RESOURCES

Finding a Therapist

Psychology Today: PsychologyToday.com

This site includes a directory to help you find a therapist near you or who specializes in your concern.

Support Helplines

1 in 6 24/7 Helpline Chat: 1in6.org/helpline

This is a dedicated helpline for boys, men, and their loved ones for assistance in overcoming sexual assault. You can also visit their website for more resources.

National Domestic Violence Hotline: 1-800-799-7233 or text "START" TO 88788

This helpline provides essential tools and support to help survivors of domestic violence so they can live their lives free of abuse. You can also visit their website at TheHotline.org.

National Sexual Assault Hotline: 1-800-656-4673

This helpline connects survivors of sexual assault with resources and local service providers. You can also visit their website RAINN.org for more information.

National Suicide Prevention Lifeline: 1-800-273-8255

This helpline provides emotional support for anyone feeling overwhelmed or depressed or in crisis. You can also visit their website SuicidePreventionLifeline.org for more resources.

Trans Hotlines at Psych Central: PsychCentral.com/blog/trans-hotline

At this website you can choose from a list of helplines for trans, nonbinary, and gender-expansive individuals.

SAMHSA National Helpline: 1-800-662-4357

This helpline connects individuals and families facing mental and/or substance use disorders with resources and services. You can find more information on their website SAMHSA.gov.

Podcasts

Black Girls Heal, hosted by Shena Tubbs

This podcast was created to help women of color break out of cycles of unhealthy relationships with unavailable partners and to address feelings of not being enough by combining coaching, therapeutic support, and practical tools.

Boundaries.me, hosted by Dr. Henry Cloud

This podcast features stories about setting healthy boundaries from writers, psychologists, leaders, and inspiring individuals.

UnF*ck Your Brain, hosted by Kara Loewentheil

This podcast offers support for women who struggle with anxiety, self-doubt, and imposter syndrome.

Books

Codependent No More: How to Stop Controlling Others and Start Caring for Yourself by Melody Beattie

The Complete Artist's Way: Creativity as a Spiritual Practice by Julia Cameron

The Five Love Languages: How to Express Heartfelt Commitment to Your Mate by Gary Chapman

REFERENCES

Brenner, Abigail. "7 Tips to Create Healthy Boundaries with Others." PsychologyToday .com. November 21, 2015. PsychologyToday.com/us/blog/in-flux/201511/7-tips-create -healthy-boundaries-others.

Claman, Priscilla. "Set Better Boundaries." *Harvard Business Review*. January 13, 2021. HBR.org/2021/01/set-better-boundaries.

Gladwell, Malcolm. *Blink: The Power of Thinking Without Thinking*. New York: Back Bay Books, 2007.

Mehl-Madrona, Lewis. *Coyote Wisdom: The Power of Story in Healing*. Rochester, VT: Bear & Company, 2005.

Mehl-Madrona, Lewis. *Healing the Mind Through the Power of Story: The Promise of Narrative Psychiatry*. Rochester, VT: Bear & Company, 2010.

Mint Life (blog). "Don't Lose Money to Burnout by Setting Boundaries at Work." Intuit Mint. Last modified October 21, 2021. Mint.Intuit.com/blog/early-career/setting-boundaries-at-work.

National Alliance on Mental Illness (NAMI). "Maintaining a Healthy Relationship." Accessed December 18, 2021. NAMI.org/Your-Journey/Family-Members-and -Caregivers/Maintaining-a-Healthy-Relationship.

Pattemore, Chantelle. "10 Ways to Build and Preserve Better Boundaries." PsychCentral.com. Last modified June 2, 2021. PsychCentral.com/lib/10-way-to-build -and-preserve-better-boundaries.

Selva, Joaquín. "How to Set Healthy Boundaries: 10 Examples + PDF Worksheets." PositivePsychology.com. August 12, 2021. PositivePsychology.com/great-self-care -setting-healthy-boundaries.

ACKNOWLEDGMENTS

Thank you to all who support me and believed in me even when I didn't believe in myself. A special thank you to Yolanda and Jim. I've been blessed to have parents who encouraged me to reach for everything I desire in life. I'd also like to recognize my clients, whom I am constantly in awe of. You remind me how resilient we all can be, and of the value of learning and loving ourselves through our story.

ABOUT THE AUTHOR

 Jaime Reeves, MA, LMFT, is a marriage and family therapist in private practice in Los Angeles, where she splits her time between walking with clients on their journey of healing, and holding seminars and workshops on cultural diversity, empowerment, and so much more. She has been a guest on podcasts like *The Spicy Life* and offers resources and tools through her organization I Am/I Rise. In her downtime, she enjoys traveling and immersing herself in cultures around the world. You can find out more about Jaime's practice at JaimeReevesPsychotherapy.com or on Instagram: @JaimeLMFT.